COOKING
International Cuisine
with Reese

TERESA A. BURNETT

Copyright © 2023 Teresa A. Burnett.

All rights reserved. No part of this book may be reproduced, stored, or transmitted by any means—whether auditory, graphic, mechanical, or electronic—without written permission of both publisher and author, except in the case of brief excerpts used in critical articles and reviews. Unauthorized reproduction of any part of this work is illegal and is punishable by law.

ISBN: 979-8-88640-923-9 (sc)
ISBN: 979-8-88640-924-6 (hc)
ISBN: 979-8-88640-925-3 (e)

Because of the dynamic nature of the Internet, any web addresses or links contained in this book may have changed since publication and may no longer be valid. The views expressed in this work are solely those of the author and do not necessarily reflect the views of the publisher, and the publisher hereby disclaims any responsibility for them.

One Galleria Blvd., Suite 1900, Metairie, LA 70001
1-888-421-2397

Table of Contents

Spring rolls w/dipping sauce 1
Rice paper wraps w/dipping sauce..3
Dipping sauce..5
Beef Pho..7
Spices for beef Pho 9
Corned-beef & spinach stew w/sardines, green beans, peas, & corn 11
Beef empanadas 13
Braised ox-tails w/butter beans & carrots...15
Steak fajitas w/saute vegetables & avocado spread 17
Chicken enchiladas 19
Baked garlic, ginger, & soy chicken 21
Curry chicken w/potatoes & carrots...23
Reese's version of Haitian's chicken in sauce...25
Italian sausages w/ peppers, onions, & mushrooms 27
Fried rice 29
Reese's Jollof rice w/corned-beef, sardines, corn, & peas..31
Reese's fiesta rice 33
Rice & beans..35
Rice & peas 37
Reese's creamy Rasta pasta 39
Reese's spaghetti Olio 41
Creamy broccoli Alfredo 43
Shrimp scampi 45
Creamy garlic Parmesan pasta w/peas...47
Chunky Guacamole..49
Avocado spread..51
Sofrito 53
Reese's version of "Epis"...55
Creamy seafood chowder 57
Reese's palm-nut soup...59
Reese's cow heel or pig feet soup..61
Okra & spinach stew 63
Reese's version of Sancocho w/rice 65
Caramelized fried plantains..67
Jamaican me crazy fried cabbage...69

The introduction of my journey

My name is Teresa A. Burnett. I am very happy to write this third cookbook. In 2015, I published my first cookbook titled "Cooking with Reese". In 2017, I published an electronic version of my second book titled "In the kitchen with Reese, a true southern bell", a hard copy of which was recently published.

My love of cooking started as a small girl growing up in my little home town of Brantley, Alabama. As a kid, I always watched other women cooking in their kitchens while asking questions such as "whatcha doing? whatcha making? how'd you do that? Can I watch you cook that?". I was always very pleased with their answer which was "of course you can". The love of learning and cooking continued to grow as I grew older. After graduating high school, I left home and started a whole new life in Worcester, Massachusetts, where I currently reside. I worked hard and put myself through college. I began with Culinary Arts and graduated in April 2004 from Salter College, formerly known as Salter's School. Then, later, I enrolled in Quinsigamond Community College and graduated first in May 2012 with a Certificate in Food Service Management, and later in August 2013 with an Associate's degree in Science.

Since my passion has always been my continuous love of learning and cooking, I developed a great interest in Cuisines of other cultures and countries. I am grateful to be living in the era of the internet and social media, which exposed me to different International Cuisines by amazing cooks, chefs, and food enthusiasts. In this cookbook, I am sharing with you international dishes that I customized to make them easier and cheaper to cook, while preserving their deliciousness as much as possible.

Spring rolls

INGREDIENTS

1 lb of ground pork
½ lb of raw shrimps cleaned, peeled & chopped
5 garlic cloves minced
¼ tsp of salt
¼ tsp of black pepper
¼ tsp of ground or chopped ginger
¼ tsp of garlic & herb seasonings
¼ tsp of onion powder
¼ tsp of garlic powder
1 whole raw carrot
1 handful of fresh spinach & arugula-chopped
1 bulb of Asian thin vermicelli rice noodles-cooked to soften
1 package of frozen small, medium or large spring roll pastry-thawed
1 egg beaten
Pastry brush

DIRECTIONS

Place a pot of water on top of the stove and bring to a boil. Add noodles let them sit to become soft and stringy approximately 3-5 minutes. Add noodles to a strainer and drain them from the hot water, and put them into another bowl and set them aside to cool. In another large bowl add ground pork, chopped shrimp, garlic and seasonings and set aside. Peel carrots then shred them as fine as you can and add them to the pork mixture, along with the chopped spinach and arugula. Use a pair of scissors and begin cutting noodles as fine as you can then add them in with the pork, shrimp and other ingredients. Mix ingredients together so everything is incorporated and set them aside. Remove spring roll wrappers from package and carefully begin separating them as easy as you can. If you separate quickly they will rip. Cover the unused wrappers with damp paper towels or a clean towel to keep them from drying out and turning hard. Lay wrapper down like a diamond shape with the pointed ends facing north, south, east and west. Or do them like you normally fold your egg rolls to make it easy for you. Add 2 heaping spoonful of filling in the wrapper and take the point end closer to you and fold it over, then tuck it under the filling. Begin rolling till you reach almost ½ ways, then take both sides 1 at a time and join them in the middle and continue rolling till you have almost reached the end. When approaching the end, use a small pastry brush or your finger and dip it in the egg, brush the end and finish rolling to seal the wrapper closed. Set it aside and continue the same way w/the rest of the spring rolls. Fry till golden brown approximately 3-4 minutes. Deep fryer or wok frying is better for frying spring rolls. Dip in sauce and enjoy. Serve hot. Yields: Plenty.

Rice paper wraps

INGREDIENTS

½ lb of large shrimp-peeled, deveined & cleaned
½ lb or less of pork belly-sliced in bite size pieces
½ lb of raw beef-sliced thin
2 sticks of butter
2 onions-sliced
4-5 garlic cloves-sliced
1 lb bunch of cilantro-clean
1 head of lettuce-washed & dried
1 cucumber-peeled & sliced the long way
¼ tsp of garlic powder
¼ tsp of onion powder
¼ black pepper
¼ tsp of salt
¼ tsp of garlic & herb seasonings
1 pack of rice paper wraps
Bowl of hot water

DIRECTIONS

Place shrimp, pork belly, beef in a bowl and set them aside then add cold water to a medium pot and add pork belly and place it on top of the stove. Let it come up to a boil and reduce heat to a low medium simmer boil. Cook pork for 35-40 or until it is folk tender. Remove pork from the liquid and set it aside to cool. Add butter to an electric skillet or a deep wok and let it melt. Add onions and garlic then let them saute in the butter for a couple of minutes, long enough to get the onions translucent then add beef. Cook beef till it is no longer bright red, a little red is OK it will continue to cook when everything is added in the butter sauce. Add seasonings, shrimp and the cooked pork in with the beef then cook till everything is fully cooked and heated through. Serve hot. Yields: Plenty.

ASSEMBLING

Dip wrap in hot water and lay it down on a flat surface. It will become loose as it sits. Add on top of the wrap a piece of lettuce, spinach, & arugula followed by bean sprouts, cucumbers, & cilantro. Now start adding a little of the shrimp, beef, pork & some of the butter sauce. Fold like you would fold any other wrap. Vegetarian rice paper wraps omit all meats.

Dipping sauce recipe follows below.

Dipping sauce

INGREDIENTS

1 Thai red hot chili pepper-chopped
½ tbsp of chopped chives
or green scallions-green tops only
1 tbsp of minced garlic
½ tsp of minced ginger
1 tbsp of sugar
½ cup of lukewarm water-to dissolve sugar
1½-2 tbsp of fish sauce
¼ tsp of toasted sesame seeds
Cilantro leaves

DIRECTIONS

Mix all ingredients together in a small serving bowl. Fish sauce is salty so be very carefully not to over add. If sauce is too salty add a tad more warm water and let it sit to cool or place it in the refrigerator. Add pieces of cilantro to the sauce. Recipe can be doubled for more sauce volume. Yields: ½ to a cup or more.

Beef Pho

INGREDIENTS

2 lbs of beef rib roast
Spice seasonings
½ tbsp of pink or sea salt
1 lb of Asian rice stick noodles
1 lb of Thai basil
1 package of bean sprouts
3 stalks of scallions-green tops only
Thai chili peppers-chopped
1 lb bunch of fresh cilantro-cleaned
Cracked black pepper

DIRECTIONS

Place a pot of cold water on top of the stove and bring to a boil. Add noodles and cook them for 5-6 minutes. Add noodles to a colander and drain, then rinse them under hot running water and set them aside till ready to use. In a large pot add beef and sachet spice package & salt along with enough cold water to cover beef. Bring to a rolling boil and then reduce heat to a low simmering boil. Remove any scum that foams to the surface. Cover and allow beef to slow cook for 2-2½ hours or until beef is tender. Remove beef from liquid broth and place it on a cutting board to cool. Strain broth and reserve it and cut the beef in medium chunks. In your personal bowl add some of the noodles and some of the cut beef and then begin adding some of the broth, add enough to cover the noodles & beef. Top with basil, sprouts, scallions, Thai peppers, cilantro, & cracked black pepper. Yields: Plenty.

Spice recipe follows below.

Spices for beef Pho

INGREDIENTS

1 cinnamon stick
2 star anise
1 whole nutmeg
6 cloves
1½ tsp of fennel seeds
1½ tsp of coriander seeds

DIRECTIONS

Add spices to a sachet bag and seal it. Double recipe for more volume.
Yields: 1 sachet bag.

Corned-beef & spinach stew w/sardines, green beans, peas, & corn

INGREDIENTS

1 onion-sliced
1 onion-chopped
3-4 garlic cloves chopped & divided in half
1 tomato & chicken flavored bouillon cube
1-8 oz can of tomato sauce
1 large tomato-chopped
Salt to taste
Black pepper to taste
1 tbsp of crushed red pepper flakes or pepper of your choice
¼ cup of Zomi red palm oil
1 lb bag of fresh spinach-washed
½ lb of chunk beef stew meat-cooked
1-12 oz can of corn beef of your choice
1-3.75 oz can of sardines
½ cup of corn, sweet peas, green beans or mix vegetables

DIRECTIONS

Place a skillet on top of the stove and add a tbsp of oil on medium heat. Cut beef into small chunks and add it to the skillet. Cook the beef on top of the stove till beef is getting a little crispy then remove it from the skillet and place it in a bowl and set it aside. Add diced onions, garlic, bouillon cubes, tomatoes, tomato sauce and pepper into a blender and blend to a wet paste. Add the palm oil to a large skillet on medium heat and saute the sliced onions till they has started to wilt and looking a little charred around the edges, approximately 5-6 minutes. Remove the onions from the skillet and place them in a small bowl or plate and set them aside. Add the beef chunks and cook them till they are cooking to a crisp chunk and remove them and add them with the onions. Add the blended sauce to the skillet and cook until it is beginning to thicken and turning into a stew consistency or a paste approximately 6-7 minutes. Add the peas, corn, green beans, crispy beef chunks & onions then cook for 5 minutes. Add spinach and cook till it has begin to wilt. Cover and reduce heat to a low simmer and let the stew simmer for 10-15 more minutes. Adjust seasoning if needed. Serve hot. Serve over white rice. Yields 4-5 or more servings.

Beef empanadas

INGREDIENTS

½ lb. of ground beef
1 heaping tbsp of Sofrito
½ tsp of Goya's Adobo-all purpose seasoning with pepper
½ tsp of Goya's Adobo-all purpose seasoning without pepper
1 tsp of garlic powder
1 tsp of onion powder
package of Sazon seasoning
8-10 olives-cut in half
potato-cooked & diced
pack of 14 or 20 oz Goya disc
½ lb of shredded cheese
Oil-for frying

DIRECTIONS

Add ground beef in a skillet on medium heat and cook until beef is 90% done and drain. Return the beef back to the stove and add the sofrito, both adobo seasonings, garlic powder, onion powder, and sazon seasoning. Continue cooking the beef and add the olives and potatoes. When done, if needed drain the beef and add some of cheese and then mix it all in and set it aside. Line the disc as if you're on an assembly line. Start with the meat, more cheese. Spoon about 1 heaping tbsp of each onto the middle of the disk. Fold it in half so it looks like a half moon, seal the disks by adding a little water around the edges and then close them by pinching it together. Finish sealing them with the back side teeth of a fork and press down hard and slide the fork outwards to seal it tightly. It's the same procedures as if you're making apple turnovers. Add oil to a deep fryer on 350 or a deep skillet and set temperature on medium high heat. When the oil is hot and has reached it's temperature for frying, begin adding the empanadas a few at a time. Fry them for 3-4 minutes on each side. Transfer pies to paper towels to drain. Serve hot. Yields 10 servings.

Braised ox-tails w/butter beans & carrots

INGREDIENTS

3 lbs of ox-tail-washed & cleaned
¼ tsp of salt
¼ tsp of black pepper
½ tbsp of garlic powder
½ tbsp of onion powder
½ tbsp of meat tenderizer
¼ tsp of garlic & herb-all purpose seasoning
½ tbsp of no salt-all-purpose seasoning
1 scotch bonnet pepper or pepper of your choice
4-5 sprigs of fresh thyme
5 garlic cloves-sliced
2 tbsp of beef base or 2 bouillon cubes
1 onion-cut in strips
½ of a red bell pepper-cut in strips
½ of a green bell pepper-cut in strips
½ of a yellow bell pepper-cut in strips
2 carrots-cut 1 inch thick on a bias
1 can of butter beans

DIRECTIONS

Place the clean oxtails in a large bowl and season them with the seasonings then add peppers, onions, garlic, and beef base to the oxtails. Cover and place them in the refrigerator overnight to marinate. Preheat oven to 350. Add 2 heaping tbsp of oil to an oven safe skillet on top of the stove on medium high heat. Remove oxtails only and begin to brown them on all sides. Once browned add enough beef broth to barely cover them then place the whole scotch bonnet pepper, pimento berries (allspice berries) & thyme in with the oxtails. Cover, and cook them on top of the stove for 15 minutes then place them in the oven and let them continue to slow cook for 1½-2 hours. After the hours are done add the peppers, onions, carrots, butter-beans, and garlic mixtures along with any juices. Continue cooking for remainder 1 hour or until oxtails are tender and almost falling off the bones. Remove the thyme stems, bay leaves and 86 them (get rid of). Serve hot. Yields: 5-6 or more servings.

Steak fajitas w/saute vegetables & avocado spread

INGREDIENTS

2 lbs of Angus beef steak or any steak of your choice
¼ tsp of onion powder
¼ tsp of garlic powder
¼ tsp of cumin
½ tsp of chili powder
¼ tsp of garlic & herb all-purpose seasoning
¼ tsp of black pepper
¼ tsp of no salt-all purpose seasoning
½ of a red bell pepper
½ of a green bell pepper
½ of a yellow bell pepper
½ of an orange bell pepper
½ of a large onion
1 large portobello mushroom
3-4 garlic cloves
1 package of flour tortilla shells
2 tbsp of avocado oil

DIRECTIONS

Slice peppers, onions, mushrooms in thin strips, then slice the garlic cloves and place them with the other vegetables set them aside. Place the steak on a cutting board and cut it in thin strips and place it in a bowl. Season the steak with the seasonings and make sure it is well coated and set it aside. Place a cast iron skillet or any skillet of your choice on top of the stove and add the oil. Add vegetables then saute them for 5-6 minutes, just long enough for them to shrink down and become translucent and possible getting a little charred on them. Add steak to vegetables and cook till meat is no longer red approximately another 6-7 minutes. Add tortilla shells in the microwave to warm. Assembly with the avocado spread followed by the sauteed vegetables and then the steak. Serve with fresh cilantro, creamy guacamole, sour cream or salsa. Serve hot. Yields: Plenty.

Chicken enchiladas

INGREDIENTS

2 boneless chicken breast
1-8 oz package of dried chilies
1 small to medium onion-cut in chunks
3 garlic cloves chopped fine or minced
¼ tsp of salt
1 chicken & tomato bouillon cube
¼ tsp of black pepper
¼ tsp of garlic & herb seasoning
¼ tsp of onion powder
¼ tsp of garlic powder
1-12 oz package of corn tortillas
2-16 oz of cheese-shredded

DIRECTIONS

Preheat oven to 350. Season chicken and place it on a sheet pan lined with aluminum foil and bake for 20 minutes. Remove pan from oven and place chicken on a rack to cool. While chicken is cooling prepare the sauce. Cut the dried chilies open and remove the seeds. Place chilies on top of the stove in about 1½ cups of cold water. Cook till chilies are becoming soft and pliable. Remove them from the heat and set them aside to cool. Place chilies, bouillon, garlic, onions, seasonings and 1 cup of the liquid into a blended and blend till smooth. Reserve remaining liquid in case sauce is too thick. Once chicken has cooled enough to handle, shred it as fine as you can and place it in a small bowl. Remove ½ cup of sauce and place it in the bowl with the chicken. Mix them together and set it aside. Add a tbsp of oil in a skillet on top of the stove on medium high heat, and add corn tortillas. Heat them on both sides till they are pliable and not breaking into pieces. Remove and place them on a plate. Place a baking dish on the counter and add enough sauce to coat the bottom. Add 1-2 tortilla at a time in the baking dish with the sauce and coat the back and front with the sauce. Let them lay flat in the baking dish and begin topping them with some of the chicken & cheese, about 1-2 tbsp. Roll and line them in the baking dish. Make space to fit the remaining tortillas. Continue with the same procedures for the rest of the enchiladas. Add any leftover chicken, sauce and cheese on top. Bake covered for 15 minutes with foil then remove foil and continue cooking till cheese has melted and sauce is bubbling, approximately 20 more minutes. Serve with guacamole, sour cream and chopped scallions. Yields: 6-7 or more servings.

Baked garlic, ginger, & soy chicken

INGREDIENTS

2 lbs. of chicken wings, chicken thighs or chicken legs
6-7 or more garlic cloves-chopped or minced
Grated ginger or ginger paste
1 heaping tsp of 5 spice powder
1-bottle of soy sauce of choice
Cooking spray
Honey

DIRECTIONS

Preheat the oven to 350. Clean chicken and place them on paper towels to dry. Place garlic and ginger under the skin of each piece of chicken and secure with toothpicks if needed, then add them to a large bowl. Add the 5 spice powder to the soy sauce and pour it over the chicken. No need to drown the chicken in the sauce, as long as it is barely covering it, that's OK. Refrigerate the chicken overnight or up to 4 hours if using the same day, rotating the chicken in the sauce to get even coating. Line a baking pan with aluminum foil or parchment paper and spray it with cooking spray. Remove the chicken from the sauce and place them on the baking pan, along with any sauce. Bake uncovered for 30 minutes, then remove the pan from the oven and rotate it around for even cooking. Continue cooking the chicken for 10-15 more minutes and remove it from the pan, drizzle a little honey over each piece. Serve hot. Yields: 7-8 servings or more servings.

Curry chicken w/ potatoes & carrots

INGREDIENTS

2 lbs of chicken-legs, wings, breasts & thighs
¼ tsp of salt
¼ tsp of black pepper
¼ tsp of garlic & herb seasonings
¼ tsp of onion powder
¼ tsp of garlic powder
¼ tsp of ginger powder
2 tbsp of curry powder
1 onion-sliced
3 garlic cloves-chopped
2 scallions-chopped
½ of a red bell pepper-sliced
½ of a green bell pepper-sliced
4-5 thyme sprigs
6-8 allspice berries
½ tbsp of fresh ginger-chopped
1 whole scotch bonnet pepper
1 chicken & tomato bouillon cube-crushed
1 cup of coconut water
1 cup of coconut milk
2 potatoes-diced
1 carrot-peeled & diced
2 bay leaves
Oil

DIRECTIONS

Clean and rinse the chicken then place them in a large bowl. Add seasonings, 1 tbsp of the curry powder and the remaining ingredients, onions, garlic, scallions, sliced peppers, thyme, allspice berries, ginger, scotch bonnet pepper and bouillon cube. Cover and let everything marinate overnight or up to 3 hours for same day cooking. Place a large skillet on top of the stove and add about 3 tbsp of oil and turn on heat. Let it heat up and then add the remaining 1 tbsp of curry powder. Cook the curry to burn for 5-10 seconds. This will only release the flavors of the curry spice and slightly darken the color. Add only the chicken and brown it on all sides then add the vegetables and all the natural juices from the chicken. Cover and let everything begin to cook on its natural juices for about 5 minutes then add the coconut milk, coconut water, potatoes, carrots and bay leaves. Place the scotch bonnet pepper on top of the chicken if you don't want all the heat that comes with it. Allow everything to come up to a boil and recover. Reduce the heat to a low to medium simmering boil and finish cooking for the remaining 20-25 minutes. Adjust seasonings and serve hot. Yields: Plenty.

Reese's version of Haitian's chicken in sauce

INGREDIENTS

2 lbs of chicken-legs, wings, thighs, & breasts
2 tbsp of Epis sauce
¼ cup of brown sugar
½ tsp of black pepper
¼ tsp of Garlic & herb-all purpose seasoning
¼ tsp of No salt-all purpose seasoning
¼ tsp of garlic powder
¼ tsp of onion powder
¼ tsp of turmeric powder
¼ tsp of ground ginger powder
Tomato paste
1 whole scotch bonnet or pepper of choice
¼ of a red bell pepper-cut in strips
¼ of a green bell pepper-cut in strips
½ of a red onion-cut in strips
2 tbsp of grated garlic cloves
1 heaping tbsp of grated ginger
1 chicken & tomato flavored bouillon
5-6 sprigs of fresh thyme
Avocado oil

DIRECTIONS

Clean the chicken and lay them on paper towels and pat them dry. Remove the skin from the chicken breast and cut it in chunks, then add all the chicken to a large bowl. Add 2 heaping tbsp of the Epis sauce to the chicken and season them with the seasonings. Mix well and make sure each piece is well coated with the sauce, then add the bell peppers, onions, garlic, ginger and the scotch bonnet in with the chicken and toss everything together. Cover and place them in the refrigerator overnight or up to 3 hours if cooking the same day. Place a skillet on top of the stove on medium heat and add 2 tbsp of oil. When the oil is hot add the brown sugar and let it cook and begin to burn (change color) from its original brown color approximately 5-6 seconds. It will turn a dark chocolate color. Then begin adding only the chicken a few pieces at a time, reserving the vegetables for later. If needed fry in batches and do not overcrowd the skillet. Brown chicken on all sides and add a heaping tbsp of tomato paste to the skillet, cook it for about 1-2 minutes to loosen and turning into a paste consistency. Add the bell peppers, onions, garlic, ginger, scotch bonnet along with the liquids from the bowl, and 1½ cups of chicken broth or hot water. Let it come to a boil and begin to reduce down to a syrupy consistency. Reduce heat to a low simmer, cover and allow the chicken to finish cooking for 25-30 more minutes. Sit the scotch bonnet pepper on top of the chicken. Serve hot. Yields: Plenty.

"Epis" recipe below

Italian sausages w/ peppers, onions, & mushrooms

INGREDIENTS

2 lbs of sweet Italian hot or mild sausages-links or patties
½ of a green bell pepper
½ of a red bell pepper
½ of a yellow bell pepper
1 large red onion
½ lb of fresh mushrooms
2 tbsp of oil
1 package of grinder rolls or bulky rolls

DIRECTIONS

Preheat oven to 350 or an indoor grill. Cut 1-2 slits in link sausage and place them in the preheated oven. Bake for 20 minutes or add them on a grill. Cook till sausages are no longer pink and cooked completely. While the sausages are cooking prep the vegetables. Slice the peppers, onion and mushrooms in strips and set them aside. Add oil in a large skillet, add the vegetables. Cook till they are beginning to get a little charred, approximately 4-6 minutes. Remove sausages from oven and add them to the peppers and onion mixture and keep them warm till ready to use. Before assembling, slice a little slit in the side of the sub rolls if they are not already sliced for you. Place them in the microwave for a few seconds to get them warm and pliable. And if going to toast them for a little, open them and spread a tad of butter and lay them butter side down, grill till golden brown. Start with adding a little peppers, onions and mushrooms then sausages and more peppers, onions, and mushrooms on top. Serve hot. Yields 6 or more servings.

Fried rice

INGREDIENTS

4 ½ cups of cooked rice-preferably day old white rice
2 heaping tbsp of oil
½ of an onion sliced
3 garlic cloves chopped or minced
1 tbsp of grated fresh ginger
1 cup of frozen sweet peas
1 cup of carrots-diced
6 oz bag of bean sprouts
Cooking spray
½ tbsp of dark soy sauce
1 tbsp of light soy sauce
1 tbsp of oyster sauce
1 tbsp of hoisin sauce
½ tbsp of fish sauce
¼ tsp of Black vinegar
¼ tsp of Black pepper
2 eggs-scrambled
1 scallion green top only
Cracked black pepper

DIRECTIONS

Cook eggs and set them aside until ready to use. Add 2-3 tbsp of oil to a hot skillet or wok and saute onions, garlic, ginger, peas, carrots, and sprouts about 2-3 minutes. Add rice and cook till heated through then add both soy sauces, oyster, hoisin, fish sauce & vinegar. Gently mix them in the rice using either a folk or chopsticks to get well coated. Do not use a spoon to mix the rice. It will make the rice to mushy. Add eggs and heat till everything is heated through. Adjust seasonings if needed and serve hot. Garnish with scallions cracked black pepper. Yields 6 or more servings.

Reese's Jollof rice w/ corned-beef, sardines, corn, & peas

INGREDIENTS

¼ cup of red palm oil
2 large onions-1 sliced & 1 chopped
1 scotch bonnet pepper-seeds removed or pepper of your choice
2 tbsp tomato paste
4 garlic cloves chopped
3 large tomatoes-cut in chunks
2 red bell peppers-cut in chunks
Salt to taste-optional
Black pepper to taste
¼ tsp of garlic powder
¼ tsp of onion powder
¼ tsp of garlic & herb seasoning
1 tbsp of paprika
½ tbsp of curry powder
1 tbsp of ginger
1 tomato & chicken flavored bouillon cube
4 sprigs of fresh thyme or 2 tsp of dried thyme
¼ cup of stew beef cooked & cut in small chunks
3 cups of white rice
1-12 oz can of corned beef-crumbled
2 bay leaves
½ cup of frozen whole kernel corn
½ cup of frozen peas
1-8 oz can of sardines
Chicken or beef broth-if needed

DIRECTIONS

Rinse rice under cold water till it is clear and no longer cloudy, about 3 rinses, set aside. Add the chopped onions, pepper, garlic, tomato, bell peppers, ginger and seasonings to a blender and blend till you have a smooth paste. Add oil to a large heavy deep bottom pot or a Dutch oven over medium high heat. Cook beef till done and a little on the crispy side, remove from oil and place it in a bowl and set it aside. Add onions and saute until they have started to turn brown around the edges, but not burned approximately 3 minutes then reduce heat to medium. Add tomato paste to onions and cook for about 2-3 minutes to cook the bitterness from the paste, then add the tomato mixture. Let it cook till it has begin to look like a paste or stew consistency, and then add the cooked beef, rice and corned beef to the sauce. Add bay leaf and cover pot with aluminum foil and a tight fitting lid. Reduce heat to low and continue cooking rice for 15 minutes without interference, after 15 minutes remove lid & foil. Fluff rice with a fork and add the corn, peas, & sardines. Recover and cook for 20-25 more minutes or till rice is completely done. Remove bay leaves and adjust seasoning if needed. Serve hot. Yields 6 or more servings.

Reese's fiesta rice

INGREDIENTS

2 strips of red bell pepper-diced
2 strips of green bell pepper-diced
2 strips of yellow bell pepper-diced
2 strips of orange bell pepper-diced
½ of an onion-diced
2 garlic cloves-chopped
½ of a Jalapeno pepper-chopped
or ¼ tsp of red pepper flakes
2 tbsp of avocado oil
Salt to taste-optional
¼ tsp of black pepper
¼ tsp of turmeric
¼ tsp of oregano
1 tomato chicken flavored bouillon
1 tsp of chili powder
1 tsp of cumin
1 tsp of ground ginger
¼ tsp of garlic powder
¼ tsp of onion powder
2 bay leaves
1 tbsp of Sofrito
½ cup of tomatoes-diced
oz can of diced tomatoes
oz can of black beans-rinsed
1-15 oz can of whole kernel corn
3 cups of long grain rice-rinsed
3 cups of vegetable broth, chicken broth or water

DIRECTIONS

Add the oil to a rice pan or Dutch oven on top of the stove on medium high heat. Add the onions, peppers, garlic and saute for 5 minute, just long enough to let them begin to set off its aroma and becoming translucent. Add chopped tomatoes, diced tomatoes along with its juices, seasonings and the bay leaves. Cook till they are beginning to look like a paste and no longer looking watery, approximately 8 minutes. Add the black beans and corn then mix them together then let everything come to a boil, and cook for 2 minutes to allow the flavors to meddle together before adding the rice. Add the rice and enough broth/water to cover the rice and over by ½ inch and let it come to a boil to allow most of the liquid to begin to boil and evaporate a little. Once liquids have almost evaporated reduce heat to low, cover pan with aluminum foil and a tight fitting lid. Cook the rice for 15 minutes; remove the lid, foil and fluff rice around using a folk to assure even cooking. Recover and cook for 10 more minutes or until rice is suitable to your taste. When done, use a folk and fluff everything around into the rice and discard bay leaves. Serve with guacamole, slice of lime, or avocados. Serve hot. Yields: 6 or more servings.

Rice & beans

INGREDIENTS

¼ cup of oil
2 tbsp of sofrito
1 tomato-diced
2 oz of tomato sauce
1 tomato-diced
1 pkg of Goya Sazon seasoning-orange top
1 pkg of Goya ham flavored seasoning (optional)
Salt to taste-optional
Black pepper to taste
1 tomato bouillon cube or ¼ tsp of tomato bouillon powder
1 can of Gandules (pigeon peas) or black beans
3 cups of rice rinsed
4 cups of chicken broth
2 bay leaves

DIRECTIONS

Add the oil to a rice or heavy bottom pan on top of the stove on medium high heat, then add the sofrito, tomatoes and the sauce. Let them cook together until the mix has started to turn into a paste or stew consistency, then add the seasoning and mix well. Add the beans and mix to incorporate them into the sauce liquids. Add the rice and mix it into the sauce then add the broth and bay leaves, let everything come up to a boil. Allow the rice to begin to evaporate some of the liquid before reducing the heat to low. Once most of the liquid has begin to evaporate, cover the pot with aluminum foil and a tight fitting lid and cook for 15 minutes without interfering. Remove the lid and using a folk, mix the rice around and recover. Let it finish cooking for 5-10 more minutes or until rice is completely done. Remove the bay leaves and 86 it (get rid of). Serve hot and with guacamole, fried plantains, or sliced avocado. Yields 6 or more servings.

Rice & peas

INGREDIENTS

1 cup of dry red kidney beans
1 whole scotch bonnet pepper-or pepper of your choice
1 tsp of No salt-all purpose seasoning
1 tsp of Garlic & Herb-all purpose seasoning
¼ tsp of black pepper
¼ tsp of garlic powder
¼ tsp of onion powder
6-8 allspice pimiento berries
2 stalks of scallions-sliced
5 sprigs of fresh thyme
1 tbsp of fresh ginger-minced or grated
4 garlic cloves-sliced
1 vegetable flavored bouillon cube
1-11.5 fl. oz can of coconut water
1-13.5 fl. oz can of unsweetened coconut milk
2½-3 cups of Basmati rice

DIRECTIONS

Rinse beans under cold running water and place them in a large bowl with cold and soak them overnight. Add beans and the water they're soaking in along with the scotch bonnet pepper, seasonings, onions, thyme, ginger, garlic and bouillon to a pot on top of the stove. Turn on heat and cover pot then let it come up to a boil and reduce heat to a simmering boil. Let the beans cook for 45 minutes or up to 1 hour, and add the coconut water and coconut milk and let everything come back up to a boil. Add the rice and sliced onions then let it come back up to a boil on its own uncovered, then allow most of the liquid to begin to evaporated. Cover the pot with a piece of aluminum foil and the lid, then reduce heat to a low simmer to allow the rice to finish cooking for 20-25 minutes. Remove the foil and the lid then fluff the rice around with a folk. Serve hot. Yields 5 or more servings.

Reese's creamy Rasta pasta

INGREDIENTS

1 lb box of Penne pasta
1½ cup of half & half
1 can of coconut milk
½ of an onion-slice
3 garlic cloves-chopped
½ of a red bell pepper-diced
½ of a green bell pepper-diced
½ of a yellow bell pepper-diced
½ of an orange bell pepper-diced
2 tbsp of flour
2 tbsp of butter or oil
5 sprigs of thyme
¼ tsp of salt
¼ tsp of cracked black peppercorns
½ tsp of onion powder
½ tsp of garlic powder
¼ tsp of Garlic & herb-all purpose seasoning

DIRECTIONS

Cook pasta for 10-12 minutes. Drain & set it aside to completely release all its water. Saute peppers, onions & garlic until they are translucent approximately 4-5 minutes. Add flour and cook for a 1 minute to cook and remove the raw taste out of the flour. add the half & half and coconut milk. Let it come up to a boil to begin the thickening then reduce heat to a low and let the sauce come up to simmering boil on its own without interfering. Add Parmesan cheese and stir it in the sauce then add pasta. Mix everything together and add more Parmesan cheese all over the top. Serve hot. Yield: Plenty.

Reese's spaghetti Olio

INGREDIENTS

1 lb of angel hair spaghetti pasta
2 stick of real butter
1 bulb of garlic-chopped
¼ cup of olive oil
1 tbsp of garlic powder
¼ tsp of salt
¼ tsp of black pepper
¼ tsp of Garlic & herb-all purpose seasonings
Parmesan cheese-shredded
Parsley-fresh or dried
½ tsp of red pepper flakes

DIRECTIONS

Cook spaghetti according to the box method then drain and set it aside. Add butter to a pan and let it melt, then add garlic and cook till it has begin to release its aroma and starting to brown but not burning, approximately 3-4 minutes. Add olive oil and seasonings and mix well. Add spaghetti. Swirl the spaghetti around in the sauce till it is all coated. Top with some Parmesan, parsley and red pepper flakes. Serve hot. Yields: 6 or more servings.

Creamy broccoli Alfredo

INGREDIENTS

8 oz of bow-tie pasta
½ lb of fresh broccoli florets
2 tbsp of butter
3 garlic cloves-minced
2 tbsp of all purpose flour
1 cup of half & half cream
2 cup of milk
¼ tsp of Garlic & herb-all purpose seasoning
¼ tsp of No salt-all purpose seasoning
Salt to taste-optional
Black pepper to taste
½ tbsp of garlic powder
½ tbsp of onion powder
¼ tsp of ground ginger powder
½ tsp of crush red pepper flakes
½ cup of shredded mozzarella or Parmesan cheese
Feta cheese
Parsley-fresh or dried

DIRECTIONS

In a large pot add cold water and bring it to a boil then add pasta and let it cook for 8-10 minutes add broccoli florets and turn off heat. Allow broccoli to steep in the hot water for a couple of minutes. Long enough to bring out the vibrant green color of it. Remove from hot water and set it aside. In another pot on medium heat, melt butter and saute garlic for a couple of minutes add flour and cook till it's turning into a paste look, approximately 1 minute or so. Slowly whisk in the 1 cup of cream. It will start to thicken up. Do not let it come to a heavy boil, a few small bubbles is OK then add 1 cup of milk and continue stirring as it's getting more thicker continue adding the other cup of milk. Add seasonings and ½ of the cheese in with the sauce and stir. Add pasta and broccoli to the sauce. Simmer on low heat to allow everything to heat through. Sauce will continue to thicken the longer it cooks and as it sits. Gradually add more milk ½ cup at a time as needed for a creamier texture. Adding more cream will only make it thicker. Also, when preheating add milk. Top with feta and parsley. Serve hot. Yields: 5-6 servings or more.

Shrimp scampi

INGREDIENTS

1 lb of linguine

Scampi sauce

1 stick of butter
¼ cups of olive oil
1 tbsp of lemon juice
1/3 cup of white wine-any
7-8 garlic cloves-sliced
1 tbsp of grated fresh ginger
¼ tsp of cracked black pepper
¼ tsp of Garlic & herb seasoning all-purpose seasoning
¼ tsp of garlic powder
¼ tsp of onion powder
¼ tsp of dried parsley
¼ tsp of crushed red pepper flakes

DIRECTIONS

Place a pot on top of the stove and add water and salt. Bring it up to a high boil and add linguine, cook for 8-10 minutes or to your desired taste. When done pour linguine into a strainer and rinse under hot running water to remove the extra starch. Set them aside and begin making the sauce. Add a small pan on top of the stove on medium heat, add butter and oil. Let the butter melt and sauce starts to bubble. Add garlic and ginger then cook till they have become fragrant and not burning, approximately 2-3 minutes. Add lemon juice, wine and seasonings and continue cooking till sauce has started to bubble and possible started to reduce a little. Add linguine, and fold them into the sauce using a thong. Serve hot and serve with grilled shrimp then garnish with the dry parsley and red pepper flakes. Yields: 7-8 or more servings.

Creamy garlic Parmesan pasta w/peas

INGREDIENTS

2½ cups of mini penne pasta
2 tbsp of butter
3 tbsp of minced garlic
1 tbsp of fresh grated ginger
2 cups of milk
½ cup of half & half cream
1 cup of shredded Parmesan cheese
1 cup of frozen peas
½ tsp of salt
¼ tsp of cracked black peppercorns
¼ tsp of garlic & herb all purpose seasoning
½ tsp of onion powder
½ tbsp of garlic powder
¼ tsp of red pepper flakes
1 tbsp of dried parsley

DIRECTIONS

Bring a large pot of cold water, salt and 1 tbsp of oil to a boil. Add penne and cook for 10 minutes. Drain pasta and rinse them under hot running water to remove any extra starch then set them aside. Using the same pot add butter and let it melt then add garlic & ginger then let them saute for about 3 minutes or until you can smell the aroma from the garlic. Add the milk, cream and let it come up to a simmering boil. Do not let it come to a high or roaring boil because the milk & cream will curdle and start to look like sour milk. Using a whisk add in ½ cup of the Parmesan cheese, seasonings & parsley. Mix till cheese has begin to melt and has a thick consistency then add peas. Let them cook for 5 minutes before adding the shells then mix everything together. Heat till everything is hot. Adjust seasonings and top with remaining Parmesan cheese & more crushed red pepper flakes. Sauce will thicken as it sits. Add more milk if needed, adding cream will only make It thicker. Also add milk when reheating. Use the whole 16 oz of penne for larger volume and double the ingredients. Yields: 5-6 or servings.

Chunky Guacamole

INGREDIENTS

2 large ripen avocados
1 bunch of fresh cilantro-cleaned
½ cup of diced red onion
½ tbsp of lime or lemon juice
3-4 garlic cloves-minced
Salt to taste-optional
Black pepper to taste
1 tsp of chopped jalapeno peppers
or crushed red pepper flakes

DIRECTIONS

Cut avocado in ½ and remove the seed. In a small bowl scoop out the middle and mash it using a folk or a potato masher for a chunky guacamole. Add all ingredients and mix well. Yields: 1-2 cups.

Avocado spread

INGREDIENTS

1 ripen avocado
¼ tsp of salt
¼ tsp of black pepper
¼ tsp of garlic & herb all purpose seasoning
¼ tsp of garlic powder
¼ tsp of onion powder
2 tbsp of ice cold water
1 bunch of fresh cilantro
1 tbsp of cold lime juice
¼ tsp of chopped jalapeno or crushed red pepper flakes

DIRECTIONS

Cut avocados in half and remove the seed. Scoop out the avocado and add it in a blender along with the salt, black pepper, garlic & onion powder, ice water, cilantro and lime juice. Pulse in the blender till everything is well blended together and avocado is a little chunky. Pour avocado mixture in a bowl and add jalapeno/red pepper, then mix everything together and serve. Yields: 1½-2 cups.

Sofrito

INGREDIENTS

½ of a red bell pepper washed seeds removed & cut in chunks
½ of a green bell pepper washed seeds removed & cut in chunks
1 red onion-cut in chunks
1 bulb of garlic cloves-peeled
1 bunch of fresh cilantro-rinsed
1 bunch of Recaito leaves
2 heaping tbsp of avocado or olive oil
1 tbsp of garlic powder
1 tbsp of onion powder
½ tbsp of salt
1 tsp of black pepper

DIRECTIONS

Add all ingredients to a blender and mix until the Sofrito resembles a wet paste. Remove sauce from the blender and pour it into containers with lids and place it in the freezer. Reserve some sauce in the refrigerator. Yields: Plenty.

Reese's version of "Epis"

INGREDIENTS

1 bunch of cilantro
1 bunch of parsley
1 lb bag of baby spinach
1 green bell pepper
1 red bell pepper
1 red onion
6 stalks of scallion
6 garlic cloves
2 tbsp of fresh ginger
1 vegetable bouillon
7 cloves or 1 tsp of dry powder cloves
1 tbsp of lemon or lime juice
1 scotch bonnet-seeds removed or 1 tsp of crushed red pepper flakes
½ tsp of black pepper
¼ tsp of Garlic & herb-all purpose seasoning
¼ tsp of No salt-all purpose seasoning
¼ tsp of garlic powder
¼ tsp of onion powder
¼ tsp of ground ginger powder
¼ cup of avocado oil

DIRECTIONS

Add all ingredients to a blender and pulse to a pasty looking sauce. Pour sauce into containers with lids and freeze. Yields: 2 cups or more.

Creamy seafood chowder

INGREDIENTS

4 medium/large potatoes-peeled & diced in chunks
2-3 tbsp of butter
1 large onion diced
2 stalks of celery-chopped
3 garlic cloves-chopped
¼ cup of all purpose flour
1 cup of warm half & half cream
1 cup of warm milk
1½ heaping tbsp of clam or seafood base
1 shrimp bouillon cube
Black pepper to taste
4-6.5 oz cans of chopped clams
½ tbsp of old bay seasoning
½ lb of any size raw shrimps peeled & cleaned
½ lb of mussels
½ lb of whole clams
½ lb of scallops
3 slices of bacon cooked & crumbled
2 stalks of scallions chopped-green tops only

DIRECTIONS

Add potatoes to a pot along with just enough cold water to cover potatoes. Cover pot and bring to a boil. Reduce heat to medium low and cook potatoes for 5 minutes. Remove from heat, drain and set them aside. In a large heavy pot add butter on medium heat. When melted add onions, celery & garlic and saute till veggies are soft. Add flour and cook till it starts to looks like a paste, approximately 1-2 minutes. And then add clams, its juices and then, let it come to a low boil to thicken. Add the warm cream & milk along with the base, & seasonings. Cook 5 minutes and add potatoes. Cook for another 5 minutes and add shrimp. Cook till shrimps have turned bright pink. Do not overcook shrimps. Reduce heat to a simmer until ready to serve. Chowder will continue to thicken. If needed add more milk or clam juice to your desired thickness. Adding more cream will make it constantly become thicker. Adjust seasonings if needed. Serve and garnish with crumbled bacon, scallions & oyster crackers. Yields 6 or more servings.

Reese's palm-nut soup

INGREDIENTS

3 medium tomatoes
1 scotch bonnet pepper or ½ tsp of crushed red pepper flakes
1 large onion-cut in chunks
4-garlic cloves
1 tbsp of fresh ginger
1 tbsp of fresh turmeric-optional
1 chicken & tomato bouillon
¼ tsp of salt
½ tsp of cracked black pepper
¼ tsp of meat tenderizer
¼ tsp of garlic & herb seasoning
½ tsp of garlic powder
½ tsp of onion powder
½ tsp of minced onions
½ lb of country style ribs
½ lb of cubed beef
½ lb of cubed pork stew meat
1 lb of chicken gizzards
2 smoked herrings
14 oz can of palm butter cream base or 1 lb can cut in half.

DIRECTIONS

Score the bottom of the tomatoes into a plus sign and add them to a small pot along with a little cold water. Place the pot on top of the stove and let it come up to a boil. Boil the tomatoes for 3-4 minutes or until skin is peeling from the tomatoes. Remove them from the hot water and place them in a cold water ice water or run them under cold water. This will stop them from continuing cooking. Remove the skin from the tomatoes and cut the tomatoes in small pieces then place them along with the onions, garlic and ginger in a blender and blend till u have a smooth to chunky look and set it aside. Leave the scotch bonnet pepper whole. Season the meats and set it aside or place it in the refrigerator to marinate overnight for next day cooking and sit the scotch bonnet pepper on top of the marinating meats. Next day, remove the meats from the refrigerator 20 minutes prior to cooking to get the overnight cold chill off of them, then add the ribs, beef, pork stew meat, gizzards, herrings, the whole scotch bonnet and any juices made to a large pot and place it on the stove. Bring it up to a boil and cover pot. Allow the meats to steam in its own juices for 10 minutes, add more water if needed to finish the steaming of the meats. Add the tomato mixture and let it cook in the meats for about 15 more minutes. Add the palm butter cream and about 4 cans of hot water to the tomato mixture and meats. Bring it up to a boil and cover, then reduce the heat and let it cook on a medium simmering boil for 2 hours. Serve hot and over white rice. Yields: Plenty.

Use the whole 1 lb can if making it for a large setting. Or freeze what's left.

Reese's cow heel or pig feet soup

INGREDIENTS

½ lb of cut-up cow feet, pig feet or pigtails
1 smoked ham-hock
2 smoked turkey tails
½ lb of pig knuckles
1 cup of split peas-rinsed & soaked overnight
¼ tsp of salt
¼ tsp of black pepper
¼ tsp of ground ginger
¼ tsp of turmeric powder
1 tsp of garlic powder
1 tsp of onion powder
1 tsp of garlic & herb all purpose seasoning
1 onion-diced
1-2 stalks of celery-chopped
2 scallions-sliced
3 garlic cloves-chopped
3 sprigs of fresh thyme
1-scotch bonnet pepper
1 tbsp of grated ginger root
1 tbsp of epis
1 can of coconut milk
2 sweet potatoes-cut in chunks
2 white potatoes-cut in chunks
1 small pumpkin or butternut squash cut in chunks
1 plantain-cut in 1 inch chunks
1 carrot-cut in chunks
½ lb of cut okra

DIRECTIONS

Prep and cook the meats the day before. Strain the liquid from the meats when it's done and place it in a separate bowl. That's going to be the liquid used for the soup. Place them in the refrigerator for next day usage. Add a large pot on top of the stove and saute the onions, garlic, celery and ginger. Cook till the onions are becoming translucent and all the vegetables are releasing it aroma, then add the seasonings, green seasonings (epis), thyme and split peas. Add the liquid from the cooked meats and cover the pot. Cook till peas are beginning to look creamy approximately 15-20 minutes. Add the potatoes, pumpkin, plantain, carrots, okra and the whole scotch bonnet pepper and bring everything back to a boil. Reduce heat to a medium boil and cook for 15-20 minutes or until vegetables are becoming slight tender then add the meats. Continue cooking till soup has started to thicken, vegetables are becoming tender and the meats are heated through. Serve hot. Yields: Plenty.

Okra & spinach stew

INGREDIENTS

½ lbs of pork stew meat
½ lb of chicken gizzards
½ lb of smoke turkey tails
2 smoked herring fillets
1 scotch bonnet pepper or pepper of your choice
1 tomato bouillon cube-crumbled
1 shrimp bouillon cube-crumbled
1 tsp of onion powder
1 tsp of garlic powder
1 tsp of turmeric
1 tsp of ground ginger
¼ tsp of black pepper
¼ tsp of garlic & herb seasonings
Hot water
½ of an onion-sliced
3 garlic cloves-chopped
½ of a red bell pepper-diced
½ cup of red palm oil
1 lb of fresh okra-cut
1 lb bag of fresh baby spinach
½ lb of raw shrimp-peeled, deveined & cleaned

DIRECTIONS

Clean and season the meats with the seasonings and place them in a large bowl. Allow them to marinate overnight in the refrigerator or up to 3 hours for same day. Add pork stew, gizzards, smoke turkey, smoked herring fillets, scotch bonnet pepper and the bouillons cubes to a large pot, along with its juices, and place them on top of the stove. Bring everything to a boil and cover then let the meats and herring begin to steaming in its own juices for 35-40 minutes or until the meats are getting about 90% tender. If needed in the steaming process add some hot water to help with finishing the steaming process of the meats. While the meats are steaming place the onions, garlic, bell pepper, a little of the palm oil to a blender and pulse, leaving the vegetables a little on the chunky side then add them to the cooking meats. Let it come up to a boil and continue cooking for 10 more minutes. Add the okra, spinach, shrimp and cook till spinach has wilted and shrimp is pink approximately 5-6 more minutes. Serve hot over rice. Yields: Plenty.

Reese's version of Sancocho w/rice

INGREDIENTS

½ lb of cut-up pork shoulder, pig feet or meats of your choice
½ lb of stew beef
½ lb of pork stew meat
½ lb of cut-up chicken
1 Batata-cut in chunks
2 potatoes-cut in chunks
1 Kabocha squash-cut in chunks
1 green plantain or cooking banana-peeled & sliced
2 ears of corn broken in 3 pieces
2 bay leaves
1-large onion cut in chunks
1 bulb of garlic-peeled & sliced
1 tbsp of fresh ginger-minced
1 tbsp of Adobo
½ tsp of black pepper
½ tbsp of onion powder
½ tbsp of garlic powder
1 packages of Sazon (orange top)
1 tsp of turmeric
Sofrito
Chicken broth or hot water
Cilantro leaves

DIRECTIONS

Place batata, potatoes and squash in a bowl of cold water and set them aside. A potato peeler is easier for the chunky hard to peel vegetables. Place meats in a large bowl and season them with all the seasonings and 1 tbsp of sofrito. Mix everything together and place it in the refrigerator to marinate overnight. Next day remove the meats from the refrigerator 15 prior to cooking, then place a large pot on top of the stove on medium high heat. Add all the meats except the chicken, along with the natural juices made from the marinating meats, the bay leaves. Cover the pot and let the meats cook for 15 minutes to allow the natural juices to extract from the meats. If the liquid starts to evaporate before the 15 minutes just add a tad more broth/hot water and let it finish cooking for the remaining 15 minutes. When the minutes are up add enough broth/hot water to cover the meats and reduce the heat to a simmering boil and let them finish cooking to begin tendering up approximately 45 minutes to an hour. After the minutes are done add the chicken, onions, garlic, ginger, potatoes, carrots, batata, squash & plantain. Cover and allow everything come up to a boil. Reduce the heat to a simmering boil and let everything finish cooking, also to allow the chicken to become cooked all the way through and the vegetables are folk tender. Turn off the heat and add cilantro. Serve hot over a bed of rice and with hot buttered cornbread. Yields: Plenty.

Caramelized fried plantains

INGREDIENTS

1 large ripen plantain
2 tbsp of butter
2 tbsp of brown sugar
2 tbsp of Honey
Pinch of salt

DIRECTIONS

Peel and cut plantain in diagonal slices and set them aside. In a small skillet on medium heat add the butter. Let the butter start to brown, but not burning then add the plantains and cook for 1 minutes on each side. Remove the plantains and put them in a plate and set them aside. Add the brown sugar to the skillet and let it melt then add the plantains back in the skillet with the brown sugar and let them finish cooking until they have begin to get golden brown and form a little caramelizing charred on them. Turn plantains over and repeat the same steps for the other side. When done, drizzle honey and sprinkle a pinch of salt over them to get that sweet and salty taste. Yields 2 servings. Double recipe for more servings.

Jamaican me crazy fried cabbage

INGREDIENTS

2 tbsp of oil-olive or avocado
½ of a cabbage-shredded
½ of a red bell pepper-sliced
½ of a green bell pepper-sliced
½ of a yellow bell pepper-sliced
1 onion-sliced
½ lb of sliced portobello mushrooms
1 tbsp of fresh chopped ginger
4-garlic cloves-sliced
4-sprigs of fresh thyme
1 tomato bouillon-crumbled
¼ tsp of black pepper
½ tsp of garlic powder
½ tsp of onion powder

¼ tsp of garlic & herb seasoning
¼ tsp of soul-food seasoning
¼ tsp of crushed red pepper flakes
¼ tsp of turmeric powder
¼ tsp of ground ginger
1 carrot-shredded
oz of coconut water

DIRECTIONS

Cut cabbage in half and cut it as if you're cutting coleslaw. But do not cut it as fine as you will coleslaw. Place cabbage in a bowl and rinse it under cool water then place it in a strainer to remove excess water, set it aside. Place a large skillet or deep pot on top of the stove on medium heat and add the oil. Once heated add bell peppers, onions, mushrooms, ginger, garlic, sprigs of thyme, bouillon and seasonings. Saute till veggies are becoming translucent and releasing its aroma then add the cabbages and cover the skillet. Cook for 5 minutes to allow the cabbages to start releasing its natural waters. If the cabbages is not releasing enough of its own water add carrots and the coconut water. Cover and continue cooking cabbages for 20 minutes, remove the lid to allow some of the water to begin evaporating, and finish cooking till cabbages are becoming tender approximately 5 more minutes. Do not overcook the cabbages to where they are becoming mushy. Serve hot with fried or grilled cod filet over a bed of rice. Sprinkle the top with crushed red pepper flakes or cracked black pepper. Yields: 7-8 servings or more.

www.ingramcontent.com/pod-product-compliance
Lightning Source LLC
LaVergne TN
LVHW072128060526
838201LV00071B/4994